AUTUMN

AUTUMN

MAGDALENA ABAKANOWICZ
ANSELM KIEFER

Second Floor
AD REINHARDT
ADOLPH GOTTLIEB
ALLAN D'ARCANGELO
LARRY RIVERS

Third Floor
RUFINO TAMAYO
CLAUDIO BRAVO
FERNANDO BOTERO
TOMÁS SÁNCHEZ

www.MarlboroughNewYork.com

Marlborough

545 W. 25th Street New York 10001 212 541 4900

Marlborough Gallery was founded in 1946 following a turbulent period post World War II, and has endured many high times, and many challenging moments. With the departure from its base of 50 years on 57th Street, this will be the first season its activities will be encompassed fully in our building located at 545 W. 25th Street. This year, 2020, with the pandemic and dramatic shift in the presentation of art and the changes evident in the consumption of the story of art, this has been a confusing as well as highly challenging period. Therefore, it is with great spirit and dedication that we present to you our new season featuring Magdalena Abakanowicz with whom we have enjoyed a fruitful and enduring relationship for over 30 years, in dialogue with Anselm Kiefer, her counterpart in the interpretation of the human struggles of the 20th Century. We are grateful for the support of the Fundacja Marty Magdaleny Abakanowicz-Kosmowskiej.

Along with the Abakanowicz / Kiefer dialogue, we have revisited facets of the gallery's legacy through a second-floor presentation of Ad Reinhardt (6 exhibitions beginning in 1970), Adolph Gottlieb (4 exhibitions beginning in 1966) and Larry Rivers. On the third floor, in homage to Pierre Levai's deep committment to artists in the southern hemisphere, we have assembled an exhibition of works by Rufino Tamayo (7 exhibitions beginning in 1977), Claudio Bravo (21 exhibitions beginning in 1981), Tomás Sánchez and Fernando Botero.

We welcome your visit as we follow all of the protocols relevant to our efforts to remain safe, and we look forward to your inquiries.

Magdalena ABAKANOWICZ (1930-2017)

Works in this series were all hand-constructed in burlap

Coexistence (1), 2002 76 1/4 x 24 1/2 x 21 in. / 193.7 x 62.2 x 53.3 cm
Coexistence (2), 2002 77 x 24 1/2 x 17 in. / 195.6 x 62.2 x 43.2 cm
Coexistence (3), 2002 76 1/2 x 24 1/2 x 15 in. / 194.3 x 62.2 x 38.1 cm
Coexistence (4), 2002 75 1/2 x 22 1/2 x 15 in. / 191.8 x 57.1 x 38.1 cm
Coexistence (5), 2002 75 3/4 x 23 1/2 x 18 1/2 in. / 192.4 x 59.7 x 47 cm
Coexistence (6), 2002 78 x 26 x 21 in. / 198.1 x 66 x 53.3 cm
Coexistence (7), 2002 78 x 25 x 17 in. / 198.1 x 63.5 x 43.2 cm
Coexistence (8), 2002 70 3/4 x 22 1/2 x 14 in. / 179.7 x 57.1 x 35.6 cm
Coexistence (9), 2002 75 3/4 x 24 x 18 in. / 192.4 x 61 x 45.7 cm
Coexistence(10), 2002 75 3/4 x 26 x 19 in. / 192.4 x 66 x 48.3 cm
Coexistence(11), 2002 69 1/4 x 23 x 23 in. / 175.9 x 58.4 x 58.4 cm
Coexistence(12), 2002 85 1/2 x 25 1/2 x 24 in. / 217.2 x 64.8 x 61 cm
Coexistence(13), 2002 85 x 26 x 25 in. / 215.9 x 66 x 63.5 cm

Magdalena ABAKANOWICZ (1930-2017)
Osiel, 2005-2006
bronze, unique
89 x 22 7/8 x 35 3/8 in. / 226.1 x 58.1 x 89.9 cm

Magdalena ABAKANOWICZ (1930-2017)
Figure in an Iron House, 1989-1990
burlap, resin and iron, unique
58 1/4 x 43 3/4 x 35 in. / 148 x 111.1 x 88.9 cm

Magdalena ABAKANOWICZ (1930-2017)
From the Anatomy Cycle - Anatomy 29, 2009
burlap, wood and steel, unique
43 x 38 1/2 x 11 in. / 109.2 x 97.8 x 27.9 cm

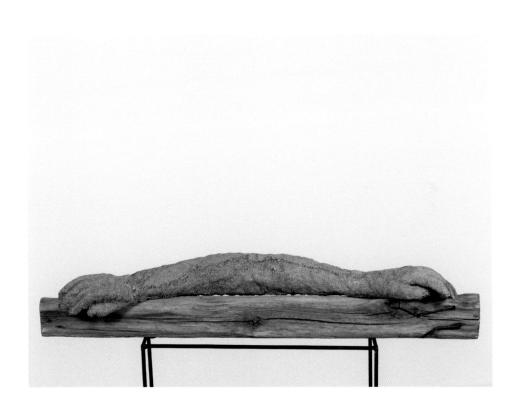

Magdalena ABAKANOWICZ (1930-2017)
Stainless Bird on Pole I, 2009
stainless steel, unique
124 x 129 7/8 x 58 in. / 315 x 330 x 150 cm

Magdalena ABAKANOWICZ (1930-2017)
Stainless Bird on Pole II, 2009
stainless steel, unique
144 1/8 x 106 1/4 x 57 1/8 in. / 366 x 270 x 145 cm

Magdalena ABAKANOWICZ (1930-2017)
Stainless Bird on Pole III, 2009
stainless steel, unique
151 5/8 x 63 x 53 1/8 in. / 385 x 160 x 135 cm

Magdalena ABAKANOWICZ (1930-2017)
Untitled, 1971-1972
sisal weaving
48 x 60 in. / 121.9 x 152.4 cm

Magdalena ABAKANOWICZ (1930-2017)
Helena, 1964-1965
wool, cotton cords, sisal, horse hair
118 x 189 in. / 300 x 480 cm

Magdalena ABAKANOWICZ (1930-2017)
Anna, 1964
woven sisal, cotton, wood, horsehair and other natural fibers
78 x 106 in. / 198.1 x 269.2 cm

Magdalena ABAKANOWICZ (1930-2017)
Vieux Rouge, 1983
sisal weaving
45 x 80 in. / 114.3 x 203.2 cm

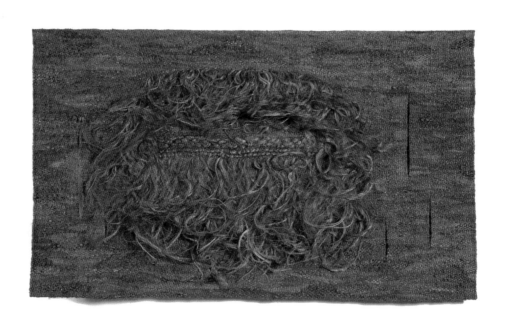

Anselm KIEFER (b. 1945)
Ich halte alle Indien in meiner Hand (I am holding all of India in my Hand), 2003
birdcages, lead, fired earth, aluminium, oil, lacquer and acrylic on canvas
75 x 110 1/2 x 12 in. / 190.5 x 280.7 x 30.5 cm
Inscribed upper left

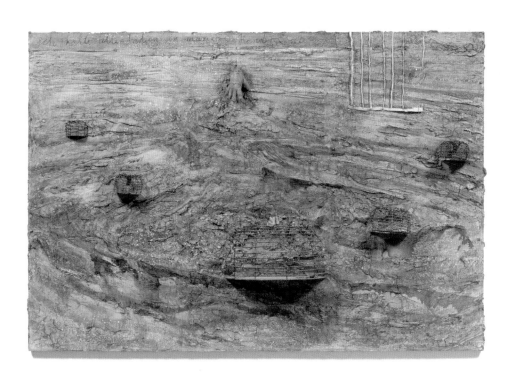

SECOND FLOOR

Ad REINHARDT (1913-1967)
Abstract Painting, 1954
oil on canvas
78 x 50 in. / 198.1 x 127 cm
signed on verso "Ad Reinhardt 'Abstract Painting,' 1954,
78 x 50 in, 732 Broadway, NYC"
Estate no. 93

Ad REINHARDT (1913-1967)
Abstract Painting, 1963
oil on canvas
60 x 60 in. / 152.4 x 152.4 cm
signed on verso "Ad Reinhardt 'Abstract Painting',
1963, 60 x 60, 732 Broadway, N York"
Estate no. 59

Ad REINHARDT (1913–1967)
Painting No. 23, 1946
oil on canvas
20 x 16 in. / 50.8 x 40.6 cm
signed on verso "Title 'Painting', Ad Reinhardt,
45 7th AV., N.Y.C."
Estate no. 219

43

Ad REINHARDT (1913-1967)
Untitled, 1947
oil on canvas
32 x 40 in. / 81.3 x 101.6 cm
Estate no. 83

Adolph GOTTLIEB (1903-1974)
Brown Field (E1), 1967
oil on canvas
60 x 72 in. / 152.4 x 182.9 cm

Adolph GOTTLIEB (1903-1974)
Flow (O5), 1969
oil on canvas
90 x 108 in. / 228.6 x 274.3 cm

49

Allan D'ARCANGELO (b. 1930)
Constellation #2, 1970
acrylic on canvas
72 x 72 in. / 182.9 x 182.9 cm
signed on verso "A D Arcangelo, nyc 1970,
'Constellation #2', 72" x 72"

Larry RIVERS (1925-2002)
Portrait of a Man (J. B. Myers), 1953-54
oil on canvas
25 x 30 3/4 in. / 63.5 x 78.1 cm

53

Larry RIVERS (1925-2002)
Head of a Woman (Berdie), 1957
oil on canvas
15 x 21 in. / 38.1 x 53.3 cm

Larry RIVERS (1925-2002)
Dutch Masters, Presidents, 1963
oil and collage on board
30 x 35 1/2 in. / 76.2 x 90.2 cm

THIRD FLOOR

Rufino TAMAYO (1899-1991)
Tres personajes, 1985
oil on canvas
49 1/4 x 71 in. / 125.1 x 180.3 cm

Claudio BRAVO (1936-2011)
Green Paper on Green Background, 2007
oil on canvas
57 1/2 x 44 7/8 in. / 146.1 x 114 cm

Claudio BRAVO (1936-2011)
Tríptico / Triptych, 2011
oil on canvas
59 x 94 1/2 in. / 149.9 x 240 cm
side panels: 59 x 23 5/8 in. / 150 x 60 cm
center panel: 59 x 47 1/4 in. / 150 x 120 cm

Fernando BOTERO (b. 1932)
Man with Book, 1998
oil on canvas
21 x 16 1/8 in. / 53.34 x 41 cm

67

Fernando BOTERO (b. 1932)
Woman on a Horse, 2008
oil on canvas
53 1/2 x 39 3/8 in. / 136 x 100 cm

Fernando BOTERO (b. 1932)
Woman on a Bed, 2009
bronze, ed. of 6
9 7/8 x 20 1/8 x 11 3/8 in. / 25.1 x 51.1 x 28.9 cm

Tomás SÁNCHEZ (b. 1948)
Inner Walker, 2019
acrylic on linen
59 x 43 1/4 in. / 150 x 110 cm

Tomás SÁNCHEZ (b. 1948)
El río va, 2020
acrylic on linen
47 3/4 x 39 in. / 121.3 x 99.1 cm

Magdalena ABAKANOWICZ
Selected Museums and Public Collections

Arkansas Arts Center, Little Rock, Arkansas
Art Institute of Chicago, Chicago, Illinois
Australian National Gallery of Art, Canberra, Australia
Birmingham Museum of Art, Birmingham, Alabama
Busan Museum of Modern Art, Busan, South Korea
Cantor Arts Center, Stanford University, Stanford, California
Caracas Museum of Modern Art, Caracas, Venezuela
Center for Contemporary Art, Warsaw, Poland
Denver Art Museum, Denver, Colorado
Des Moines Art Center, Des Moines, Iowa
Detroit Institute of Arts, Detroit, Michigan
Fondation Toms Pauli, Lausanne, Switzerland
Fondazione Pomodoro, Milan, Italy
Frederik Meijer Gardens and Sculpture Park, Grand Rapids, Michigan
Giuliano Gori Collection, Spazi d'Arte, Santomato di Pistoia, Pistoia, Italy
Grant Park, Chicago, Illinois
Grounds for Sculpture, Hamilton, New Jersey
Henie-Onstad Kunstsenter, Høvikodden, Norway
Hess Collection, Art Museum, Napa Valley, California
Hiroshima City Museum of Contemporary Art, Hiroshima, Japan
Hirshhorn Museum and Sculpture Garden, Washington, District of Columbia
Institut d'Art Contemporain, Villeurbanne, France
Israel Museum, Jerusalem, Israel
Jardin des Tuileries, Paris, France
John Kluge Collection, Charlottesville, Virginia
Kemper Museum of Contemporary Art, St. Louis, Missouri
Kunstindustrimuseet, Oslo, Norway

Kyoto National Museum of Modern Art, Kyoto, Japan
Los Angeles County Museum of Art, Los Angeles, California
Ludwig Museum, Cologne, Germany
Marwen Foundation, Chicago, Illinois
Menil Drawing Institute, Houston, Texas
Metropolitan Museum of Art, New York, New York
Milwaukee Art Museum, Milwaukee, Wisconsin
Minneapolis Institute of Art, Minneapolis, Minnesota
Musée d'Art Moderne de la Ville de Paris, Paris, France
Musée National d'Art Moderne, Centre Pompidou, Paris, France
Museo Nacional Centro de Arte Reina Sofía, Madrid, Spain
Museo Tamayo Arte Contemporáneo, Mexico City, Mexico
Museum of Arts and Design, New York, New York
Museum of Contemporary Art, Chicago, Illinois
Museum of Contemporary Art, Los Angeles, California
Museum of Contemporary Art, North Miami, Miami, Florida
Museum of Contemporary Crafts, New York, New York
Museum of Fine Arts, Houston, Texas
Museum of Modern Art, New York, New York
Museum of Modern Art, Shiga, Japan
Museum Würth, Kunzelsau, Germany
Muzeum Narodowe, Warsaw, Poland
Muzeum Sztuki, Lódz, Poland
Nagoya City Art Museum, Nagoya, Japan
Nasher Sculpture Center, Dallas, Texas
National Gallery of Art, Washington, District of Columbia
National Museum of Contemporary Art, Seoul, South Korea
National Museum of Modern Art, Busan, South Korea

National Museum of Women in the Arts, Washington, District of Columbia
National Museum, Stockholm, Sweden
Neanderthal Museum, Mettmann, Germany
Nelson-Atkins Museum of Art, Kansas City, Missouri
Noord-Brabant Provinciehuis,'s-Hertogenbosch, Netherlands
Phoenix Art Museum Sculpture Garden, Phoenix, Arizona
Portland Art Museum, Portland, Oregon
Runnymede Sculpture Farm, Woodside, California
San Francisco Museum of Modern Art, San Francisco, California
Sezon Museum of Art, Tokyo, Japan
Smart Museum of Art at The University of Chicago, Chicago, Illinois
Sonje Museum of Contemporary Art, Seoul, South Korea
Stedelijk Museum Amsterdam, Amsterdam, Netherlands
Storm King Art Center, Mountainville, New York
Toledo Art Museum, Toledo, Ohio
Virginia Museum of Fine Arts, Richmond, Virginia
Walker Art Center, Minneapolis, Minnesota
Western Washington University, Bellingham, Washington

Anselm KIEFER
Selected Museums and Public Collections

Albright-Knox Art Gallery, Buffalo, New York
Aldrich Contemporary Art Museum, Ridgefield, Connecticut
Art Gallery of New South Wales, Sydney, Australia
Art Institute of Chicago, Chicago, Illinois
Astrup Fearnley Museum of Modern Art, Oslo, Norway
Beyeler Foundation, Basel, Switzerland
The Broad, Los Angeles, California
Castello di Rivoli Museum of Contemporary Art, Torino, Italy
Cincinnati Art Museum, Cincinnati, Ohio
Cleveland Museum of Art, Cleveland, Ohio
Fundación Proa, Buenos Aires, Argentina
Groninger Museum, Groningen, Netherlands
Guggenheim Bilbao, Bilbao, Spain
Hammer Museum, Los Angeles, California
Harvard University Art Museums, Cambridge, Massachusetts
Hirshhorn Museum and Sculpture Garden, Washington, District of
Columbia
Hudson Valley Center for Contemporary Art, Peekskill, New York
Indianapolis Museum of Art, Indianapolis, Indiana
Kunstmuseum Wolfsburg, Wolfsburg, Germany
Los Angeles County Museum of Art, Los Angeles, California
Metropolitan Museum of Art, New York, New York
Milwaukee Art Museum, Milwaukee, Wisconsin
Modern Art Museum of Fort Worth, Fort Worth, Texas
Museo di Arte Moderna e Contemporanea, Trento, Italy
Museum of Contemporary Art, Chicago, Illinois
Museum of Contemporary Art, Los Angeles, California
Museum of Fine Arts, Houston, Texas

Museum of Fine Arts, Boston, Massachusetts
Museum of Modern Art, New York, New York
National Galleries of Scotland, Edinburgh, Scotland
National Gallery of Art, Washington, District of Columbia
National Gallery of Australia, Canberra, Australia
North Carolina Museum of Art, Raleigh, North Carolina
Peggy Guggenheim Collection, Venice, Italy
Philadelphia Museum of Art, Philadelphia, Pennsylvania
Reina Sofía Museum, Madrid, Spain
Royal Museums of Fine Arts of Belgium, Brussels, Belgium
San Francisco Museum of Modern Art, San Francisco, California
Serralves Foundation Museum of Contemporary Art, Porto, Portugal
Solomon R. Guggenheim Museum, New York, New York
Stedelijk Museum of Modern Art, Amsterdam, Netherlands
Stedelijk Museum voor Actuele Kunst, Ghent, Belgium
Tate Gallery, London, England
Tel Aviv Museum of Art, Tel Aviv, Israel
Toledo Museum of Art, Toledo, Ohio
University of Iowa Museum of Art, Iowa City, Iowa
Virginia Museum of Fine Arts, Richmond, Virginia
Walker Art Center, Minneapolis, Minnesota
Wallraf-Richartz Museum, Cologne, Germany

Ad REINHARDT
Selected Museums and Public Collections

Ackland Art Museum at the University of North Carolina, Chapel Hill, North Carolina
Akron Museum of Art, Akron, Ohio
Allen Art Museum at Oberlin College, Oberlin, Ohio
Art Institute of Chicago, Chicago, Illinois
Brooklyn Museum, Brooklyn, New York
Canton Museum of Art, Canton, Ohio
Cleveland Museum of Art, Cleveland, Ohio
Fondazione Pomodoro, Milan, Italy
Giuliano Gori Collection, Spazi d'Arte, Santomato di Pistoia, Pistoia, Italy
Harvard University Art Museums, Cambridge, Massachusetts
Henie-Onstad Kunstsenter, Høvikodden, Norway
Hirshhorn Museum and Sculpture Garden, Washington, District of Columbia
Indianapolis Museum of Art, Indianapolis, Indiana
Kawamura Memorial Museum of Art, Sakura, Japan
Lauren Rogers Museum of Art, Laurel, Mississippi
Memorial Art Gallery of the University of Rochester, Rochester, New York
Mildred Lane Kemper Art Museum, St. Louis, Missouri
Minneapolis Institute of Arts, Minneapolis, Minnesota
Modern Art Museum of Fort Worth, Fort Worth, Texas
Museum of Contemporary Art, Chicago, Illinois
Museum of Contemporary Art, Los Angeles, California
Museum of Modern Art, New York, New York
National Gallery of Art, Washington, District of Columbia
National Gallery of Australia, Canberra, Australia
North Carolina Museum of Art, Raleigh, North Carolina
Philadelphia Museum of Art, Philadelphia, Pennsylvania

Princeton University Art Museum, Princeton, New Jersey
Rhode Island School of Design Museum of Art, Providence, Rhode Island
Smithsonian Archives of American Art, Washington, District of Columbia
Solomon R. Guggenheim Museum, New York, New York
Tate Gallery, London, United Kingdom
University of Iowa Museum of Art, Iowa City, Iowa
Walker Art Center, Minneapolis, Minnesota
Whitney Museum of American Art, New York, New York
Wilhelm Lehmbruck Museum, Duisburg, Germany
William H. Van Every Gallery, Davidson College, Davidson, North Carolina
Yale University Art Gallery, New Haven, Connecticut

Adolph GOTTLIEB
Selected Museums and Public Collections

Block Museum of Art, Northwestern University, Evanston, Illinois
Butler Institute of American Art, Youngstown, Ohio
Everson Museum of Art, Syracuse, New York
Flint Institute of Arts, Flint, Michigan
Fogg Art Museum, Harvard University, Cambridge, Massachusetts
Fort Wayne Museum of Art, Fort Wayne, Indiana
Fred Jones Jr. Museum of Art, University of Oklahoma, Norman, Oklahoma
Frederick R. Weisman Art Foundation, Los Angeles, California
Frost Art Museum, Florida International University, Miami, Florida
Grey Art Gallery, New York University, New York, New York
Guild Hall, East Hampton, New York
Hakone Open-Air Museum, Hakone, Japan
Hammer Museum, UCLA Grunwald Center for Graphic Arts, California
Herbert F. Johnson Museum of Art, Cornell University, Ithaca, New York
High Museum of Art, Atlanta, Georgia
Hirshhorn Museum and Sculpture Garden, Washington, District of Columbia
Hood Museum of Art, Dartmouth College, Hanover, New Hampshire
Hyde Collection Art Museum, Glens Falls, New York
Indianapolis Museum of Art, Indianapolis, Indiana
Irish Museum of Modern Art, Dublin, Ireland
Israel Museum, Jerusalem, Israel
IVAM Centre Julio Gonzalez, Valencia, Spain
Jack S. Blanton Museum of Art, The University of Texas, Austin, Texas
Jewish Museum, New York, New York
John and Mabel Ringling Museum of Art, Sarasota, Florida
Krannert Art Museum, University of Illinois, Champaign, Illinois

Lauren Rogers Museum of Art, Laurel, Mississippi
Los Angeles County Museum of Art, Los Angeles, California
Lowe Art Museum, University of Miami, Coral Gables, Florida
Metropolitan Museum of Art, New York, New York
Miami Art Museum, Miami, Florida
Midwest Museum of Art, Indianapolis, Indiana
Milwaukee Art Museum, Milwaukee, Wisconsin
Minneapolis Institute of Art, Minneapolis, Minnesota
Mobile Museum of Art, Mobile, Alabama
Modern Art Museum of Fort Worth, Fort Worth, Texas
Montana Museum of Art and Culture, Missoula, Montana
Montclair Art Institute, Montclair, New Jersey
Munson-Williams-Proctor Institute, Utica, New York
Musée d'Art Contemporain de Montréal, Montréal, Canada
Musée National d'Art Moderne, Centre National d'Art et de Culture
Georges Pompidou, Paris, France
Museo Nacional Centro de Arte Reina Sofia, Madrid
Museum of Contemporary Art, Los Angeles, California
Museum of Ein Harod, Ein Harod, Israel
Museum of Fine Arts, Boston, Massachusetts
Museum of Fine Arts, Houston, Texas
Museum of Frieder Burda, Baden, Baden, Germany
Museum of Modern Art, New York, New York
National Gallery of Art, Washington, District of Columbia
Nelson-Atkins Museum of Art, Kansas City, Missouri
Neuberger Museum of Art, State University of New York at Purchase,
Purchase, New York
Neue Nationalgalerie, Berlin, Germany

New Britain Museum, New Britain, Connecticut
Newark Museum, Newark, New Jersey
New Orleans Museum of Art, New Orleans, Louisiana
North Carolina Museum of Art, Raleigh, North Carolina
Norton Museum of Art, West Palm Beach, Florida
Orlando Museum of Art, Orlando, Florida
Peggy Guggenheim Collection, Venice, Italy
Pennsylvania Academy of the Fine Arts, Philadelphia, Pennsylvania
Philadelphia Museum of Art, Philadelphia, Pennsylvania
Philbrook Museum of Art, Tulsa, Oklahoma
Phillips Collection, Washington, District of Columbia
Picker Art Gallery, Colgate University, Hamilton, New York
Plattsburgh State Art Museum, Plattsburgh, New York
Pomona College Museum of Art, Claremont, California
Portland Art Museum, Portland, Oregon
Power Gallery of Contemporary Art, Museum of Contemporary Art
Australia, Sydney, Australia
Princeton University Art Museum, Princeton, New Jersey
Provincetown Art Association and Museum, Provincetown,
Massachusetts
Rhode Island School of Design Museum of Art, Providence, Rhode
Island
Rose Art Museum, Brandeis University, Waltham, Massachusetts
Saint Louis Art Museum, St. Louis, Missouri
San Francisco Museum of Modern Art, San Francisco, California
Santa Barbara Museum of Art, Santa Barbara, California
Seattle Art Museum, Seattle, Washington
Sheldon Memorial Art Gallery, University of Nebraska, Lincoln, Nebraska

Smart Museum of Art at The University of Chicago, Chicago, Illinois
Smith College Museum of Art, Northhampton, Massachusetts
Smithsonian American Art Museum, Washington, District of Columbia
Snite Museum of Art, University of Notre Dame Art Gallery, Notre Dame, Indiana
Solomon R. Guggenheim Museum, New York, New York
Spencer Museum of Art, University of Kansas, Lawrence, Kansas
Stanford University, Cantor Center for Visual Arts, Stanford, California
Storm King Art Center, Mountainville, New York
Syracuse University Art Collection, Syracuse, New York
Tacoma Art Museum, Tacoma, Washington
Tamagawa University Education Museum, Tamagawa, Japan
Tampa Museum of Art, Tampa, Florida
Tate Gallery, London, England
Tehran Museum, Tehran, Iran
Tel Aviv Museum, Tel Aviv, Israel
Toledo Museum of Art, Toledo, Ohio
Tweed Museum of Art, University of Minnesota, Duluth, Minnesota
Ulrich Museum of Art, Wichita State University, Wichita, Kansas
University Art Museum at California State University, Long Beach, California
University Art Museum at University of Albany, Albany, New York
University of Iowa Museum of Art, Iowa City, Iowa
University of Lethbridge Art Gallery, Lethbridge, Alberta, Canada
University of Michigan Museum of Art, Ann Arbor, Michigan
University of Missouri-Columbia, Museum of Art and Archaeology, Columbia, Missouri
University of South Florida Art Museum, Tampa, Florida

University of Wyoming Art Museum, Laramie, Wyoming
Victoria and Albert Museum, London, England
Virginia Museum of Fine Arts, Richmond, Virginia
Walker Art Center, Minneapolis, Minnesota
Whitney Museum of American Art, New York, New York
Wichita Art Museum, Wichita, Kansas
Worcester Art Museum, Worcester, Massachusetts
Wright Museum of Art at Beloit College, Beloit, Wisconsin
Yale University Art Gallery, New Haven, Connecticut

MARLBOROUGH NEW YORK
545 WEST 25TH STREET
NEW YORK, NY 10001
212 541 4900

DOUGLAS KENT WALLA, CEO — dkwalla@marlboroughgallery.com
MEGHAN BOYLE KIRTLEY, Administrator — boyle@marlboroughgallery.com
ALEXA BURZINSKI, Gallery Director — burzinski@marlboroughgallery.com
GREG O'CONNOR — greg@marlboroughgallery.com
DiBOMBA KAZADI, Bookkeeper — kazadi@marlboroughgallery.com

SEBASTIAN SARMIENTO, Director — sarmiento@marlboroughgallery.com
DIANA BURROUGHS, Director & Graphics — burroughs@marlboroughgallery.com
NICOLE SISTI, Sales Assistant — sisti@marlboroughgallery.com

BIANCA CLARK, Co-Registrar — clark@marlboroughgallery.com
AMY CAULFIELD, Co-Registrar — caulfield@marlboroughgallery.com
LUKAS HALL, Archivist — hall@marlboroughgallery.com
ROBERT RICHBURG, Facilities Manager — richburg@marlboroughgallery.com
REN PAN, Content provider — pan@marlboroughgallery.com

JOHN WILLIS, Buchanan Manager — willis@marlboroughgallery.com
ANTHONY NICI, Master crater — mnywarehouse@marlboroughgallery.com
MATT CASTILLO, Art Handler — mnywarehouse@marlboroughgallery.com
JEFF SERINO, Installations — mnywarehouse@marlboroughgallery.com
PETER PARK, Installations — park@marlboroughgallery.com

MARLBOROUGH FINE ART (LONDON)
6 ALBEMARLE STREET
MAYFAIR
LONDON W1S 4BY
UNITED KINGDOM
+44 20 7629 5161

John Erle Drax, Chairman — Erle-Drax@marlboroughgallery.com
Mary Miller, Director
Geoffrey Parton, Director — Parton@marlboroughgallery.com
Frankie Rossi, Managing Director — Rossi@marlboroughgallery.com
Debbie Lowe, Assistant to Head of Accounts
Angela Trevatt, Head of Accounts — Trevatt@marlboroughgallery.com
Joe Balfour, Head of Graphics and sales Director
Jessica Draper, Sales Director
Laura Langeluddecke, Executive assistant
Mike Pollard, Registrar
Erin Sleeper, Social Media and Digital manager
Morgan Ward, Sales and Exhibitions — Ward@marlboroughgallery.com
Will Wright, Associate Director

GALERÍA MARLBOROUGH MADRID
ORFILA, 5
28010 MADRID
SPAIN
+34 91 319 1414

Anne Barthe, Sales Director — abarthe@gameriamarlborough.com
Belén Herrera Ottino, Sales Director — bherrera@galeriamarlborough.com
Claudia Manzano, Sales — cmanzano@galeriamarlborough.com
Nerea Pérez, Press, Auctions — nperez@galeriamarlborough.com
Nieves Rubiño, Director of Finance, Legal and HR — nrubino@galeriamarlborough.com
Germán Lucas, Finance Assistant — glucas@galeriamarlborough.com
Cynthia González, Registrar — cgonzalez@galeriamarlborough.com
Jara Herranz, Catalogues, Archives — jherranz@galeriamarlborough.com
Noemí Morena, Reception — nmorena@galeriamarlborough.com
Fermín Rosado, Warehouse — frosado@galeriamarlborough.com
Juan García, Warehouse — jgarcia@galeriamarlborough.com

GALERÍA MARLBOROUGH BARCELONA
C/ ENRIC GRANADOS, 68
08008 BARCELONA
+34 93 467 44 54

Mercedes Ros, Director, Sales, Public Relations — mros@galeriamarlborough.com
Laura Rodríguez, Registrar, Press, Sales, Reception — lrodriguez@galeriamarlborough.com
Ester García, Catalogues, Press, Reception — eguntin@galeriamarlborough.com

Design: Dana Martin-Strebel
Installation Photo Credits: Pierre Le Hors
Editor: Nicole Sisti
Research: Lukas Hall

ISBN 978-1-7358170-0-2

Edition of 1000
Printed in China by Permanent Press